ULYSSES S. *Grant*

ULYSSES S. *Grant*

OUR EIGHTEENTH PRESIDENT

By Ann Graham Gaines

SPIRIT
of America™

The Child's World®, Inc.
Chanhassen, Minnesota

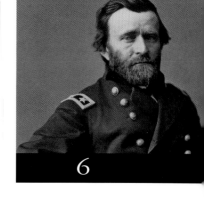

6

ULYSSES S. *Grant*

Published in the United States of America by The Child's World®, Inc.
PO Box 326 • Chanhassen, MN 55317-0326 • 800-599-READ • www.childsworld.com

Acknowledgments
The Creative Spark: Mary Francis-DeMarois, Project Director; Elizabeth Sirimarco Budd, Series Editor; Robert Court, Design and Art Direction; Janine Graham, Page Layout; Jennifer Moyers, Production

The Child's World®, Inc.: Mary Berendes, Publishing Director; Red Line Editorial, Fact Research; Cindy Klingel, Curriculum Advisor; Robert Noyed, Historical Advisor

Photos
Cover: White House Collection, courtesy White House Historical Association; Appomattox: National Museum of American Art, Washington, DC/Art Resource, NY: 18; Bettmann/Corbis: 25; Chicago Historical Society: 14, 16 (P&S-1920.1645; Artist: Paul Phillipateaux), 23 (P&S-1971.0177; Artist: Alonzo Chappel); Ulysses S. Grant photographs from the collection of James A. Bultema: 6, 9, 10, 12, 13, 17, 19, 20, 24, 21, 26, 27, 30, 33; Library of Congress Collections: 11, 22, 23, 28, 35, 36, 37; The New York Public Library: 29; Ohio Historical Society: 7, 8

Library of Congress Cataloging-in-Publication Data
Gaines, Ann.
  Ulysses S. Grant : our eighteenth president / by Ann Graham Gaines.
    p. cm.
  Includes bibliographical references and index.
  ISBN 1-56766-855-0 (library bound : alk. paper)
  1. Grant, Ulysses S. (Ulysses Simpson), 1822–1885—Juvenile literature. 2. Presidents—United States—Biography—Juvenile literature. [1. Grant, Ulysses S. (Ulysses Simpson), 1822–1885. 2. Presidents.] I. Title.
  E672 .G2 2001
  973.8'2'092—dc21

                                        00-011455

Contents

Chapter ONE

The Beginning

Ulysses S. Grant is known as an outstanding general who led the Northern states to victory during the Civil War. When Americans chose him as their president in 1868, they hoped he would be a great leader for the country as well.

ULYSSES S. GRANT WAS A GREAT ARMY GENERAL and the nation's 18th president. He was born on April 27, 1822, in Point Pleasant, Ohio. Grant's parents, Hanna and Jesse, owned a small farm. They raised horses, pigs, and cows and also grew vegetables and fruit.

Jesse Grant worked as a tanner, someone who makes animal hides into leather. When Ulysses was born, his father worked in another tanner's shop. In 1823, the Grant family moved to Georgetown and started a new farm. The family cleared many trees from their land and then sold the wood for lumber. Jesse also opened a tannery of his own. Over time, he sold so many hides that he became a rich man.

As a child, Ulysses worked in his father's tannery, but he did not like this work. He

liked farming much better. Even as a very young boy, Ulysses enjoyed taking care of the family's horses. He handled them so well that by age eight, he could drive a pair of horses hitched to a wagon.

Ulysses was always very smart. He began attending a one-room schoolhouse in Georgetown. He discovered that he liked to read and was also good at math. When he had learned all he could at the tiny school, Ulysses's parents sent him away to stay at a private school. Soon he had completed his high school education.

In 1839, Ulysses was accepted to the U.S. Military Academy at West Point. Attending West Point is a great honor. The school only

Jesse Root Grant (left) was a tanner who made a great deal of money. He and his son were very different. While Ulysses was shy and quiet, Jesse could be a loud and boastful person. Ulysses' mother, Hanna (right) once told a reporter what her son had been like as a child. "He was always a steady, serious sort of boy, who took everything in earnest; even when he played, he made a business of it."

Interesting Facts

▶ The first book Ulysses S. Grant ever read was a biography of George Washington.

After the Grants moved to Georgetown, Jesse opened the tannery shown at right. He often asked his sons to help him there, but Ulysses would do almost anything to avoid it. "He would rather do anything else under the sun than work in the tannery," Jesse once said of his son.

accepts excellent students. When Ulysses enrolled there, he was 17 years old. He had reached his full height, standing just over five feet, seven inches tall. As a young man, he was very slim.

Ulysses did not think he wanted a career in the army. He went to West Point to please his father. But once there, Ulysses worked hard and found that he liked it. West Point offered regular college classes in subjects such as literature and mathematics. Its students also studied military subjects, such as military **strategy.** Outside of the classroom, students learned to march and handle weapons properly. Life wasn't always easy at West Point, but graduates from the school were strong young men who were prepared to fight for their country.

When he graduated, Ulysses Grant planned to spend just a few years in the army. His goal for the future was to become a math teacher. But first, like all other West Point graduates, he became an army **officer.**

Grant went to Texas just before the United States went to war against Mexico in 1846. His **regiment** was then sent to Mexico, where it fought many battles. Grant became well known for his bravery. After the Americans captured the Mexican capital, Mexico City, the war ended. Grant was **promoted** to first lieutenant because of his excellent fighting during the war.

In 1848, Grant went to Missouri to marry Julia Boggs Dent, whom he had met five years earlier. Her parents gave the couple land near St. Louis as a wedding present. Over the next few years, the army assigned Grant to one post

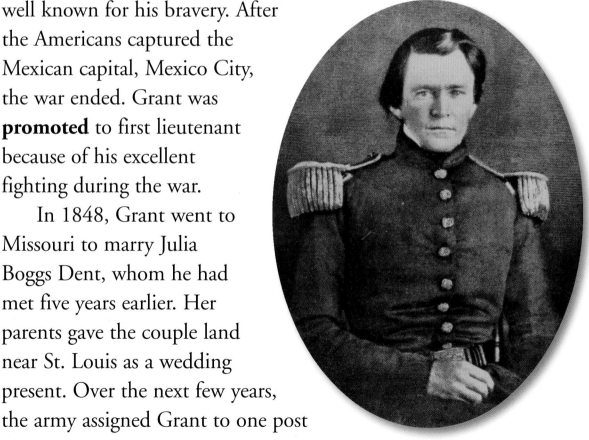

This is the earliest known photograph of Grant. It was taken shortly after he graduated from West Point, when he was a second lieutenant in the infantry.

This rare photograph was taken of Grant (at left) in May of 1845 at Camp Salubrity, Louisiana. On the right is Alexander Hayes, a close friend of Grant's at West Point and his comrade during the Mexican War. Hayes, by then a brigadier general, was killed during the Civil War.

after another. In 1852, he was transferred to California. By then Grant and Julia had two young sons. Rather than moving the whole family to California, Julia and the children stayed in Missouri with her relatives.

Grant missed his wife and family very much. He became so lonely that he started to drink heavily. He spent his free time in saloons. His commanding officer finally forced Grant to leave the army in 1854 because of his drinking problem. But Grant would not be out of the military for long.

IN 1848, JULIA DENT AND ULYSSES S. GRANT MARRIED. AT THE TIME, SHE HAD no idea that she would one day become first lady of the United States. Her new husband had no dreams of entering politics, the work of the government.

Julia's parents had been pioneers. They moved from the East to St. Louis, Missouri, where she was born in 1826. Her father was a rich farmer, and the Dent family lived in luxury. They owned slaves who cooked, worked in their fields, and kept their house clean. Julia received a fine education for a girl of her day. In 1843, at age 17, she graduated from a private school. That was also the year she met Ulysses Grant.

Julia's brother had attended West Point, and Grant had been one of his classmates. When Grant was assigned to a military post in St. Louis, he visited Julia's brother. The Dents often invited Grant back, and he and Julia soon fell in love. They married in 1848, after Grant returned from the Mexican War.

The early years of their marriage were difficult for Julia. Her husband did not make as much money as her father did. She had four children, eight years apart. The army transferred Grant from post to post, and Julia was usually left behind. During the Civil War, she feared for her husband's life. But through good times and bad, Grant was always devoted to her. "Since I have loved Julia, I have loved no one else," he once wrote. Theirs was a strong, happy marriage. In fact, their four children agreed that they never saw a cross word spoken between them.

11

Chapter TWO

Civil War

In 1854, Grant returned to his farm and family in St. Louis. But he joined the army again in 1861 to fight in the Civil War. He is shown here at about the time the war began.

GRANT WAS HAPPY TO LEAVE CALIFORNIA. He returned to St. Louis and his family. That year, he built a four-room log cabin on the land he and Julia had received as a wedding present. Over the next few years, Grant farmed their land, as well as that of his father-in-law. But he never made much money. He also bought and sold land, but he was not successful at this business either.

After Julia's mother died, the Grants decided to leave Missouri. In 1860, Grant's younger brother offered him a job as a clerk in the family hardware and leather store in Galena, Illinois. The family moved there so Grant could take the job.

Just 11 months later, the Civil War began. Southern states had **seceded** from the **Union**

Grant built this home in St. Louis for his family in the 1850s. He hoped to run a successful farm, but he had little luck. He named their new farm "Hardscrabble," which means a place with soil so poor that almost nothing can grow in it.

and formed their own country. They called it the Confederate States of America. President Abraham Lincoln finally decided it was worth going to war to bring the Southern states back into the Union. Grant agreed with Lincoln. In 1861, he left his job at the hardware store and joined the Union army.

The governor of Illinois made Grant the commander of a regiment of volunteer troops. Most of his men were young and had little experience, but he trained them well. Soon they became excellent soldiers. Grant impressed his commanders so much that he was promoted to brigadier general within four months.

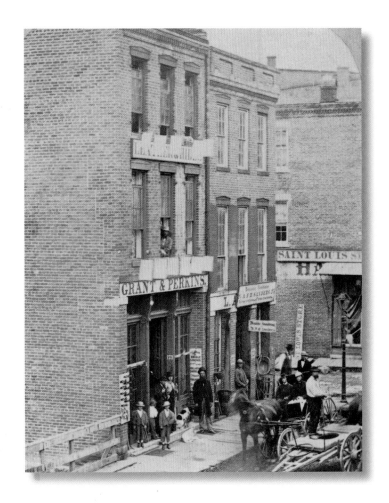

Before the start of the Civil War, Grant worked at his family's hardware and leather goods store in Galena, Illinois.

On February 6, 1862, Grant and his men won a battle at Fort Henry, Tennessee. Ten days later, they won the first major Union victory of the war. Grant's soldiers attacked Fort Donelson in Tennessee. It became clear to the Confederate soldiers stationed there that they had no chance of winning. All 15,000 Confederates **surrendered** to Grant.

President Abraham Lincoln rejoiced at the news. He praised Grant and promoted him to major general. Grant became a national hero. Americans nicknamed him "Unconditional Surrender." This was because he liked to end a battle only when the enemy had given up completely.

After these victories, Grant remained with his troops in Tennessee. On April 6, 1862, he and his men were surprised by a large number of Confederate soldiers at Shiloh Church. The Battle of Shiloh followed. Grant displayed great courage there. His fierce fighting inspired his men to fight hard, too. But the Union finally lost that terrible two-day battle. Many Union soldiers died or were wounded there. Afterward, some Union army officials wanted Lincoln to fire Grant. But Lincoln refused to do so. He explained, "I can't spare this man. He fights." Lincoln realized Grant was not to be blamed for what had happened at Shiloh. He put Grant in command of all Western forces.

General Grant's army invaded western Tennessee in 1862. After Union soldiers defeated the Confederates at Fort Donelson, the Union took control of western Tennessee and Nashville. This was Grant's first major success during the war.

After Shiloh, Grant marched his men south. Confederate soldiers had built fortifications at Vicksburg, Mississippi. Vicksburg was a place of great importance to the Confederates. As long as they controlled it, they could ship goods up and down the Mississippi River. It also allowed them to communicate quickly by sending messengers up the river. Grant was determined to take Vicksburg.

After months of fighting, the Confederate soldiers surrendered to Grant on July 4, 1863. He took another 20,000 Confederate soldiers prisoner. This victory split the Confederate States of America in two because it could no longer use the Mississippi River. It made it difficult for the Confederate government and its army to function.

In March of 1864, Lincoln named Grant general in chief of the entire Union army. Grant made plans for the rest of the war. He ordered General William Tecumseh Sherman to fight through the South. Grant fought in and around Virginia. Time and again, his soldiers battled Confederate General Robert E. Lee's Army of Northern Virginia. The soldiers on both sides fought very hard.

Nevertheless, Grant wore down General Lee and his men bit by bit. Tens of thousands of Union and Confederate soldiers fell in battle, dead or wounded. But the Union army was bigger. Lee finally had to surrender to Grant.

Lee and Grant met at Appomattox Courthouse on the morning of April 9, 1865. Grant offered the Confederates generous terms of surrender. Lee had been afraid that thousands of Confederate soldiers might be tried for **treason** and hung. But Grant simply required them to lay down their arms and promise to fight no more. President Lincoln was pleased with the terms Grant offered. He wanted to see the South treated in a kind and fair way. Other Americans thought Grant had not punished the Confederates severely enough, however. Many people believed the South was to blame for the terrible war. After all, they had rebelled against the Union.

Grant's troops took a brief rest on May 21, 1864, at their temporary head-quarters near Massaponax Church, Virginia. General Ulysses S. Grant is shown at left leaning over the shoulder of General Meade. The two men were consulting a map as they prepared to attack Robert E. Lee's forces. It would be nearly a year before Grant's men could force Lee's army to surrender.

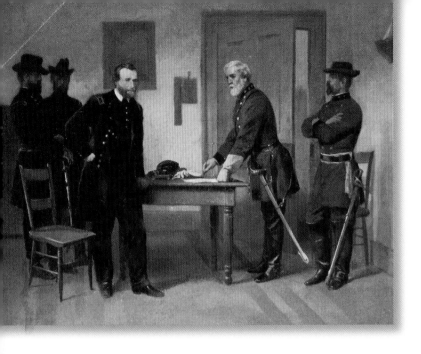

Confederate General Robert E. Lee surrendered to Grant on April 9, 1865. Grant later wrote about the event: "I said to Lee that I hoped and believed this would be the close of the war; that it was most important that the men should go home and go to work."

Interesting Facts

▶ For every soldier killed in battle during the Civil War, two died of disease.

▶ Grant was very thin during the war, weighing only 135 pounds.

The Civil War continued for a short time after Lee's surrender. Union General Sherman burned Richmond, the capital of the Confederate States of America. This ended fighting in the South. Confederate President Jefferson Davis was soon captured. There were a few more small battles in the west, but the last Confederate soldiers laid down their arms on June 23, 1865.

Throughout much of the war, Grant's wife and youngest children lived in Illinois. Toward the end of the war, they moved to New Jersey. He visited them whenever he could. In April of 1865, after the surrender at Appomattox, Grant reported to Lincoln in Washington, D.C. Lincoln invited him to stay and go to the theater with him one night. Grant refused. He wanted very much to see his family. Had he accepted, he would have been in Ford's Theater the night that John Wilkes Booth **assassinated** President Lincoln.

18

DURING THE CIVIL WAR, ULYSSES S. GRANT AND ABRAHAM LINCOLN developed a great loyalty and respect for one another. At the beginning of the war, Abraham Lincoln had few generals upon whom he could depend. He knew little about Ulysses Grant until the Confederates in Vicksburg, Mississippi, surrendered. Lincoln then realized that Grant was a great leader, a man he could count on to fight to the end. After Lincoln put Grant in charge of all Union armies, the United States began to defeat the Confederate States of America.

Lincoln and Grant met several times during the war. Grant visited Lincoln in the White House to discuss war plans. Lincoln visited Grant's camp on the battlefield. They were both quiet, thoughtful men who listened to one another. As the North came closer to victory, Americans thanked both the great general and the president for saving the Union.

Chapter THREE

After the War

At the close of the Civil War, General Grant was considered a great hero. Still, the war had been violent, taking the lives of many young men. Some of Grant's victories had been among the bloodiest.

HISTORIANS HAVE DESCRIBED THE CIVIL WAR as the bloodiest war in the history of the United States. More than 600,000 soldiers died. That number included 350,000 Northerners and 250,000 Southerners. Cities and towns in the North had suffered little damage during the war because few battles had taken place there. But there had been many battles in the South, and much of it lay in ruins. Union soldiers had taken Southern farmers' crops and equipment. Abraham Lincoln had declared all Southern slaves free during the war. When the Civil War ended, slave owners had no choice but to release the people whom they had held in bondage.

The term **Reconstruction** is used to describe the period during which the Union

AL TO THE CHIEF WHO IN TRIUMPH ADVANCES."

Grant had lived in Galena for only a year before the Civil War began. Few people knew him at the time, but by the end of the war, he was famous. Cheering citizens greeted him upon his return.

was restored. Lincoln had wanted to make the South's return to the Union as easy as possible. He thought Southerners should be allowed to decide many matters for themselves. One thing he believed was that the Southern states should decide how and when to give equal rights to blacks.

Some members of Lincoln's **political party,** the Republicans, thought the South deserved to be punished. These men called themselves the Radical Republicans. They did not want former Confederates to be allowed to hold any political office. They also wanted

After the war, much of the South was in ruins. Men, women, and children in every Southern state were starving. Not only was there little food to eat, but there was no money, no livestock, and no seed to plant new crops. People's homes and other buildings were destroyed. Now Union leaders had to decide how much help to give these states that most Northerners blamed for starting the war.

the former slaves to be granted **civil rights** at once. These views became popular with many people in the North.

When Lincoln was assassinated, his vice president, Andrew Johnson, became president. Johnson was a Southerner, but he never supported the states that had seceded from the Union. He had always remained loyal to the United States. Once the war was over, however, he wanted to help the South. Like Lincoln, he wanted to let the Southern states

22

govern themselves. But as a Southerner, he did not believe that the former slaves deserved the same rights as white people. Johnson was a member of the Democratic Party, which had ideas very different from those of the Republicans. From the start, Johnson fought fiercely against the Radical Republicans in Congress.

In 1866, Congress passed the 14th **Amendment** to the U.S. **Constitution.** This granted civil rights to all persons born in the United States. It also said no state could take away these rights. Blacks were finally recognized as citizens. Congress decided only Southern states that ratified, or approved, the 14th Amendment would be readmitted to the Union. In 1867, Congress passed the Reconstruction Act. This law put the U.S. military in charge of Southern states.

During this period, Ulysses Grant remained in the army. He toured the South on behalf of the government, talking about reconstruction. Grant did not think the South should be punished harshly.

President Andrew Johnson was a Southerner, and he wanted to help the South rebuild itself after the war. But many members of Congress wanted to punish the Confederates. They could not agree with Johnson about how to go about the process of reconstruction. In the end, Johnson was an unpopular president.

He wanted to see it become strong and stable once more, believing it was the only way to restore the Union. Still, Grant did differ with many Southerners—and President Johnson—on one point. He fully supported giving black men the right to vote. (At the time, no women were allowed to vote.)

In 1867, Grant was also the secretary of war, an advisor to the president, for a short time. He replaced Edwin M. Stanton, whom President Johnson had fired. Congress later gave back Stanton's job, saying he had been unfairly dismissed. Grant stepped down from his position without complaint. His decision to leave peacefully, without making a fuss, made President Johnson angry. Johnson wanted Grant to insist that the job was his.

When it was time for another election, most people did not want Andrew Johnson to run for president. His party, the Democrats, chose another man as their **candidate.** The Republicans hoped they could convince Grant to run for office. He had been a hero to the public during the Civil War and was still extremely popular. In 1868, the Republican Party chose Grant as its presidential candidate, and he won the election that November.

▶ Julia Grant's family owned slaves. In fact, her father once gave Ulysses Grant a slave named William Jones. Grant could have made money by selling Jones. Instead, he signed a document that gave Jones his freedom.

▶ As a young man, Grant had no interest in **politics.** He never dreamed of holding any public office. The death of Abraham Lincoln changed his mind. Many people felt that Grant was the only person who could reunite the nation after the Civil War.

A campaign ribbon from the election of 1868 shows Ulysses S. Grant with the vice presidential candidate, Schuyler Colfax.

Chapter FOUR

The Presidency

Grant won the election of 1868 by about 300,000 votes. Black men had cast more than 500,000 votes for him, helping to decide the election. At the time, black men did not yet have the guaranteed right to vote.

ULYSSES S. GRANT WAS **INAUGURATED** THE 18th president of the United States in 1869. Unfortunately, few things went well for President Grant. **Scandals** plagued his presidency and hurt his reputation. Although he was an honest man, many people close to him were not.

During President Grant's first year in office, two men, James Fisk and Jay Gould, planned to corner the gold market. They wanted to buy all the gold in the United States so they could control its price. Their plan was illegal.

For their plan to work, the government's gold would have to be kept off the market. They paid Grant's brother-in-law to do just that, hoping his power with the president

would help. When Grant heard about the plan, he knew he had to stop it. He ordered that $4 million of government gold be put on the market and sold. Unfortunately, this greatly lowered the price of gold. People who owned it lost a great deal of money, and they blamed President Grant.

The president tried to make people forget about the scandal by returning his attention to the most important issue of the day: Reconstruction. One of his main goals was to help black Americans. As a general, Grant had fought

At his inauguration, Grant said he hoped to renew a spirit of good will among all people in the United States. He knew the reconstruction of the South would be the most serious issue of his term.

Even after slavery was made illegal, life for African Americans in the South was difficult. Many, like the people shown in this photograph, worked on the same farms as they had when they were slaves, earning barely enough money to survive. President Grant did what he could to help them, but his efforts accomplished little.

alongside black soldiers. He had helped slaves gain their freedom. As president, he hoped to ensure that they would never lose it again.

A few positive things happened during Grant's presidency. One was the 15th Amendment. This 1870 addition to the Constitution granted black men the right to vote. Black men had voted in the previous election, but this amendment promised that this right could never be taken away. Grant

also won passage of a number of **bills** that helped enforce civil rights for blacks. One was the Force Act of 1870, which said the government could send its troops to the South if anyone tried to stop black men from voting.

Another bill that Grant supported was the Ku Klux Klan Act of 1871. The Ku Klux Klan was a group of white men that used violence—beatings, whippings, and even murder—to control blacks. Local governments and police wouldn't do anything to stop this. In fact, some leaders and police were even members of the Klan. The Ku Klux Klan Act said troops could be sent to the South to stop the Klan. Unfortunately, this was effective only as long as the troops stayed in the South. As soon as they left, blacks were again victims of violence and hatred.

The Ku Klux Klan was a hate group started in 1866 in Tennessee. Its members used threats and violence to keep blacks from gaining equal rights as U.S. citizens.

Grant, his youngest son Jesse, and his wife Julia posed for this portrait during his presidency. Some people said the Grants spoiled their children, especially Jesse and the second youngest, Nellie. But most of all, they were simply a happy family. One friend said, "I have never seen a case of greater domestic happiness than existed in the Grant family."

Grant tried to convince Americans that Southern white men should not have total control of their state governments. Unfortunately, he failed, and white men again dominated the South. White Southerners passed laws known as the Black Codes. These laws prevented blacks from living as fully free people. They also made sure that whites had all the power and that blacks remained poor and landless. The lives of former slaves were little better than they had been during the time of slavery.

In 1871, Grant was able to celebrate an achievement. The United States signed the **Treaty** of Washington with Great Britain, which required the British to pay the United States $15 million. This was to pay for damage the Confederates, using ships built in Britain, had done to the Union during the Civil War. This was Grant's only success in dealings with other countries.

When Andrew Johnson was president, the United States had purchased Alaska from Russia. Many Americans wanted to see the United States grow even bigger. Grant wanted the United States to take over Santo Domingo on the Caribbean island of Hispaniola. He thought this would increase American trade in the Caribbean Sea. He also thought Southern blacks might want to settle there. But Congress rejected the treaty. Today Santo Domingo is the nation of the Dominican Republic.

In 1872, more scandals surfaced. Some of Grant's closest advisors were involved. The worst involved the transcontinental railroad.

This coast-to-coast railroad had cost the nation nearly $3 billion. The owners of a construction company, called Crédit Mobilier of America, wanted to keep some of the money for themselves. They overcharged the government for work the company did on the transcontinental railroad. Then they stole the money.

Unfortunately, Grant's vice president, Schuyler Colfax, was accused of accepting money from Crédit Mobilier. With the election of 1872 drawing near, Grant had to choose a new vice presidential candidate.

Even with all these problems, the American people believed that Grant was an honest man. His supporters convinced voters that he had nothing to do with the scandals. In the election of 1872, Grant won a second term of office. His new vice president was Henry Wilson.

Throughout Grant's presidency, the nation had money problems. For one thing, the government was still paying for the Civil War. In addition, the massive railroad project was draining funds from both the government and from private sources. Things grew more serious during his second term. In the fall of 1873, many banks went out of business. Soon many small companies were forced to close as well. A **depression** began that lasted for five years. Millions of Americans lost their jobs.

As the nation suffered through the depression, the public learned of more scandals in the government. The secretary of the treasury, William Richardson, placed a close friend in charge of collecting overdue **taxes.** Richardson made a deal that allowed his friend to keep half of what he collected for himself. By the time anyone found out, the tax agent had pocketed $200,000.

Other problems surfaced as well. Grant's personal secretary accepted bribes from liquor companies that did not want to pay whiskey taxes. Grant's secretary of war was involved in the illegal sale of Native American trading posts. While these government workers were using their power to get richer,

Voters expected Grant to be a strong president because of his record during the Civil War. Unfortunately, he was unable to muster the bold leadership that had made him a great general.

the rest of the nation was still suffering through the terrible depression.

Through all of the scandals, one other law was passed to help black Americans. The Civil Rights Act of 1875 said that whites could no longer keep blacks out of public places, such as hotels, restaurants, and theaters. Unfortunately, this law had little effect because no one enforced it. In 1883, the Supreme Court decided it went against the laws of the U.S. Constitution.

Grant left office in 1877, knowing that he had not been a successful president. He and Julia went on a round-the-world tour that lasted more than two years. By the time Grant arrived back home, he was popular once again. In 1880, many Republicans hoped Grant would run for president a third time. After 35 **ballots,** Republicans chose James A. Garfield as their candidate instead.

After that, Grant and his wife moved to New York City. He invested in various businesses. In 1884, one firm in which he had invested went out of business. Grant had huge debts. He worried about how to provide for his family. He took the advice

Interesting Facts

▸ During her father's presidency, the Grants' daughter, Nellie, was married in a ceremony at the White House.

34

The Grants traveled the world at the end of his presidency. They are shown here (seated third and fourth from left) at a temple in Luxor, Egypt.

of his close friend, the famous author Mark Twain, who suggested that Grant write his **memoirs** to earn money. Twain believed many people would want to read about Grant's life as a military leader and politician.

Grant's bad luck continued, however. Just as he began writing his book, tragedy struck. While eating a piece of fruit, he grabbed his throat in pain. After being examined by his doctor, Grant learned that he had cancer of the throat. A lifetime of cigar smoking had caught up with him.

Grant's health grew weaker, but he was determined to finish his memoirs. He completed his work in the summer of 1885. He died on July 23, just one week after putting down his pen. Americans mourned his death and honored his heroism during the Civil War. Today he is remembered as a weak president but as a great general who helped to restore the Union in a time of crisis.

Grant's health grew steadily worse after he learned he had throat cancer. As he struggled to finish his memoirs, he often felt too sick to do anything else. "There cannot be a hope of going far beyond this time," he said. "It is nearly impossible for me to swallow. It pains me even to talk."

DURING RECONSTRUCTION, SOUTHERN STATES WERE FORCED TO PERMIT black men to vote. But many Northern states still denied them the right. In 1869, Congress voted in favor of the 15th Amendment to the U.S. Constitution. It stated that suffrage (the right to vote) could not be denied because of race, color, or "previous condition of servitude." The amendment became law in March of 1870. Four Southern states had ratified the amendment only because they would not have been permitted to rejoin the Union otherwise.

Even after the amendment was passed, black men continued to be denied the right to vote. This was because some states passed laws stating that men had to own property or pass a literacy test to be able to vote. In other places, blacks were threatened with violence if they attempted to vote. The 15th Amendment did not prohibit such voting restrictions. It also did not extend the right to vote to black women. At that time, no women were allowed to vote in the United States. Women had already begun to fight for the right, but they would have to continue to do so for years. The 19th Amendment, which gave women the right to vote, was finally approved in 1920.

1822 Ulysses S. Grant is born on April 27 in Point Pleasant, Ohio.

1828 At age 6, Grant starts school.

1839 Grant enrolls at the U.S. Military Academy, West Point, at age 17.

1843 Grant graduates from West Point at age 21.

1846 After being assigned to several different army posts, Grant fights in the Mexican War.

1848 The Mexican War ends. Grant travels to St. Louis, Missouri, where he marries his sweetheart, Julia Dent.

1852 The army stations Grant at a fort in California. He misses his family terribly and drinks to ease his loneliness.

1854 Grant resigns from the army. He returns to St. Louis and his family. They start a farm.

1860 Since leaving the army, Grant has failed at one venture after another. He moves his family to Galena, Illinois, where he becomes a clerk in the hardware and leather store owned by his family.

1861 The Civil War begins. Grant joins the Union army.

1862 On February 6, Grant and the men under his command win a small battle at Fort Henry, Tennessee. Ten days later, they win the first major Union victory of the war. About 15,000 Confederate soldiers surrender to Grant at Fort Donelson on the Cumberland River in Tennessee. In April, he suffers terrible defeat at the Battle of Shiloh.

1863 Thousands of Confederate soldiers surrender to Grant after his siege of Vicksburg, Mississippi.

1864 Lincoln appoints Grant general in chief of the Union army.

1865 On April 9, Confederate general Robert E. Lee surrenders to Grant at Appomattox Courthouse in Virginia. President Lincoln is assassinated five days later.

1866 After the war, Grant is named general of the armies of the United States. Congress passes the 14th Amendment to the U.S. Constitution, granting civil rights to all persons born in the United States.

1867 Congress passes the Reconstruction Act, which puts the U.S. military in charge of Southern states. Grant is briefly President Johnson's secretary of war.

1868 The Republican political party nominates Grant as their presidential candidate. He wins the election.

1869 Grant is inaugurated as president of the United States. In May, the transcontinental railroad is completed. James Fisk and Jay Gould plan to corner the gold market with the aid of President Grant's brother-in-law. Grant learns of the plan and takes action to stop it. This is the first of many scandals during Grant's time in office.

1870 The 15th Amendment is ratified, giving black men the right to vote. The Force Act is passed, which allows the government to send troops to the South if anyone attempts to stop black men from voting.

1871 The Ku Klux Klan Act is passed, allowing the government to send troops to the South to stop the Klan from committing violent acts. The United States and Great Britain sign the Treaty of Washington.

1872 Grant's vice president is accused of taking bribes in the Crédit Mobilier scandal. Grant must select a new vice presidential candidate, Henry Wilson, for the upcoming election. Grant is elected to a second term.

1873 A depression begins that lasts five years. Millions of Americans lose their jobs as companies go out of business.

1875 The Civil Rights Act says that whites cannot keep blacks out of public places, such as hotels, restaurants, and theaters. The law is not enforced.

1877 Grant leaves office. He and his wife, Julia, depart on a round-the-world tour that lasts two years.

1880 Some Republicans encourage Grant to run for president again, but James Garfield is chosen to run as the Republican candidate instead.

1884 Grant starts to write his memoirs. He is diagnosed with cancer of the throat.

1885 Ulysses S. Grant completes his memoirs only a week before he dies on July 23. Mark Twain ensures that Grant's work is published. It becomes a best-seller.

amendment (uh-MEND-ment)
An amendment is a change or addition made to the Constitution or other documents. Congress passed the 14th Amendment in 1866.

assassinate (uh-SASS-ih-nayt)
Assassinate means to murder some-one, especially a well-known person. John Wilkes Booth assassinated President Lincoln in 1865.

ballots (BA-luts)
A ballot is a round of voting. After 35 ballots, Republicans in 1880 chose James Garfield instead of Grant as their presidential candidate.

bills (BILZ)
Bills are ideas for new laws that are presented to a group of lawmakers. Grant encouraged Congress to pass bills to help black people.

candidate (KAN-dih-det)
A candidate is a person running in an election. In 1868, the Republican Party chose Grant as its presidential candidate.

civil rights (SIH-vel RYTZ)
Civil rights are the rights guaranteed by the Constitution to all citizens of the United States. Radical Republicans wanted blacks to have civil rights.

constitution (kon-stih-TOO-shun)
A constitution is the set of basic principles that govern a state, country, or society. The U.S. Constitution includes the principles that govern the United States.

depression (deh-PRESH-un)
A depression is a period of time in which there is little business activity, and many people are out of work. A depression began in 1873 that lasted for five years.

inaugurate (ih-NAWG-yuh-rayt)
When politicians are inaugurated, they formally enter an elected office. Grant was inaugurated the 18th president in 1869.

memoirs (MEM-wahrz)
Memoirs are a written account of a person's life. Grant wrote his memoirs in the last year of his life.

officer (AW-feh-ser)
An officer is a leader in the military who commands other soldiers. Grant became an officer after graduating from West point.

political party (puh-LIT-ih-kul PAR-tee)
A political party is a group of people who share similar ideas about how to run a government. Lincoln and Grant were both members of the Republican political party.

politics (PAWL-ih-tiks)
Politics refers to the actions and practices of the government. Grant had no interest in politics as a young man.

promoted (pruh-MOH-tid)
People who are promoted receive a more important job or position to recognize their good work. Grant was promoted in the army because of his excellent fighting during the war.

reconstruction (ree-kun-STRUK-shun)
Reconstruction is the rebuilding of something. The period in history after the Civil War is known as Reconstruction because the nation was trying to rebuild the Union.

regiment (REJ-ih-ment)
A regiment is a group of soldiers led by a colonel. Grant was part of a regiment that was sent to Mexico during the Mexican War.

scandals (SKAN-delz)
Scandals are shameful actions that shock the public. Scandals plagued Grant's presidency.

secede (suh-SEED)
If a group secedes, it separates from a larger group. The Southern states seceded from the Union in 1860 and 1861.

strategy (STRAT-eh-jee)
In the military, strategy is the science of planning and directing movements and operations. Students at West Point study military strategy.

surrender (suh-REN-dur)
If an army surrenders, it gives up to its enemy. A Confederate army of 15,000 soldiers surrendered to Grant at Fort Donelson.

taxes (TAK-sez)
Taxes are sums of money that citizens pay to support their government. A scandal involving taxes occurred during Grant's presidency.

treason (TREE-zun)
Treason is the act of hurting one's country or helping its enemies. General Lee worried that Confederate soldiers would be tried for treason.

treaty (TREE-tee)
A treaty is a formal agreement between nations. The United States signed the Treaty of Washington with Great Britain in 1871.

Union (YOON-yen)
The Union is another name for the United States. During the Civil War, the Northern states were called the Union.

Our Presidents

President	Birthplace	Life Span	Presidency	Political Party	First Lady
George Washington	Virginia	1732–1799	1789–1797	None	Martha Dandridge Custis Washington
John Adams	Massachusetts	1735–1826	1797–1801	Federalist	Abigail Smith Adams
Thomas Jefferson	Virginia	1743–1826	1801–1809	Democratic-Republican	widower
James Madison	Virginia	1751–1836	1809–1817	Democratic Republican	Dolley Payne Todd Madison
James Monroe	Virginia	1758–1831	1817–1825	Democratic Republican	Elizabeth Kortright Monroe
John Quincy Adams	Massachusetts	1767–1848	1825–1829	Democratic-Republican	Louisa Johnson Adams
Andrew Jackson	South Carolina	1767–1845	1829–1837	Democrat	widower
Martin Van Buren	New York	1782–1862	1837–1841	Democrat	widower
William H. Harrison	Virginia	1773–1841	1841	Whig	Anna Symmes Harrison
John Tyler	Virginia	1790–1862	1841–1845	Whig	Letitia Christian Tyler / Julia Gardiner Tyler
James K. Polk	North Carolina	1795–1849	1845–1849	Democrat	Sarah Childress Polk

42

President	Birthplace	Life Span	Presidency	Political Party	First Lady
Zachary Taylor	Virginia	1784–1850	1849–1850	Whig	Margaret Mackall Smith Taylor
Millard Fillmore	New York	1800–1874	1850–1853	Whig	Abigail Powers Fillmore
Franklin Pierce	New Hampshire	1804–1869	1853–1857	Democrat	Jane Means Appleton Pierce
James Buchanan	Pennsylvania	1791–1868	1857–1861	Democrat	never married
Abraham Lincoln	Kentucky	1809–1865	1861–1865	Republican	Mary Todd Lincoln
Andrew Johnson	North Carolina	1808–1875	1865–1869	Democrat	Eliza McCardle Johnson
Ulysses S. Grant	Ohio	1822–1885	1869–1877	Republican	Julia Dent Grant
Rutherford B. Hayes	Ohio	1822–1893	1877–1881	Republican	Lucy Webb Hayes
James A. Garfield	Ohio	1831–1881	1881	Republican	Lucretia Rudolph Garfield
Chester A. Arthur	Vermont	1829–1886	1881–1885	Republican	widower
Grover Cleveland	New Jersey	1837–1908	1885–1889	Democrat	Frances Folsom Cleveland

President	Birthplace	Life Span	Presidency	Political Party	First Lady
Benjamin Harrison	Ohio	1833–1901	1889–1893	Republican	Caroline Scott Harrison
Grover Cleveland	New Jersey	1837–1908	1893–1897	Democrat	Frances Folsom Cleveland
William McKinley	Ohio	1843–1901	1897–1901	Republican	Ida Saxton McKinley
Theodore Roosevelt	New York	1858–1919	1901–1909	Republican	Edith Kermit Carow Roosevelt
William H. Taft	Ohio	1857–1930	1909–1913	Republican	Helen Herron Taft
Woodrow Wilson	Virginia	1856–1924	1913–1921	Democrat	Ellen L. Axson Wilson Edith Bolling Galt Wilson
Warren G. Harding	Ohio	1865–1923	1921–1923	Republican	Florence Kling De Wolfe Harding
Calvin Coolidge	Vermont	1872–1933	1923–1929	Republican	Grace Goodhue Coolidge
Herbert C. Hoover	Iowa	1874–1964	1929–1933	Republican	Lou Henry Hoover
Franklin D. Roosevelt	New York	1882–1945	1933–1945	Democrat	Anna Eleanor Roosevelt Roosevelt
Harry S. Truman	Missouri	1884–1972	1945–1953	Democrat	Elizabeth Wallace Truman

Our PRESIDENTS

President	Birthplace	Life Span	Presidency	Political Party	First Lady
Dwight D. Eisenhower	Texas	1890–1969	1953–1961	Republican	Mary "Mamie" Doud Eisenhower
John F. Kennedy	Massachusetts	1917–1963	1961–1963	Democrat	Jacqueline Bouvier Kennedy
Lyndon B. Johnson	Texas	1908–1973	1963–1969	Democrat	Claudia Alta Taylor Johnson
Richard M. Nixon	California	1913–1994	1969–1974	Republican	Thelma Catherine Ryan Nixon
Gerald Ford	Nebraska	1913–	1974–1977	Republican	Elizabeth "Betty" Bloomer Warren Ford
James Carter	Georgia	1924–	1977–1981	Democrat	Rosalynn Smith Carter
Ronald Reagan	Illinois	1911–	1981–1989	Republican	Nancy Davis Reagan
George Bush	Massachusetts	1924–	1989–1993	Republican	Barbara Pierce Bush
William Clinton	Arkansas	1946–	1993–2001	Democrat	Hillary Rodham Clinton
George W. Bush	Connecticut	1946–	2001–	Republican	Laura Welch Bush

Presidential FACTS

Qualifications
To run for president, a candidate must
- be at least 35 years old
- be a citizen who was born in the United States
- have lived in the United States for 14 years

Term of Office
A president's term of office is four years. No president can stay in office for more than two terms.

Election Date
The presidential election takes place every four years on the first Tuesday of November.

Inauguration Date
Presidents are inaugurated on January 20.

Oath of Office
I do solemnly swear I will faithfully execute the office of the President of the United States and will to the best of my ability preserve, protect, and defend the Constitution of the United States.

Write a Letter to the President
One of the best things about being a U.S. citizen is that Americans get to participate in their government. They can speak out if they feel government leaders aren't doing their jobs. They can also praise leaders who are going the extra mile. Do you have something you'd like the president to do? Should the president worry more about the environment and encourage people to recycle? Should the government spend more money on our schools? You can write a letter to the president to say how you feel!

1600 Pennsylvania Avenue
Washington, D.C. 20500

You can even send an e-mail to: president@whitehouse.gov

For Further INFORMATION

Internet Sites

Visit these Web sites about Ulysses S. Grant:
http://www.mscomm.com/~ulysses/
http://saints.css.edu/mkelsey/student.html

Find more information about Ulysses S. Grant's years at school:
http://www.ohiohistory.org/places/grantsch/

Find out more about the farm Grant started after he came home from California:
http://www.grantsfarm.com/

Learn more about Grant's victory at Vicksburg, Mississippi, during the Civil War:
http://www.nps.gov/vick

Find more information about Robert E. Lee's surrender:
http://www.nps.gov/apco/

Visit the Ulysses S. Grant National Historic Site in St. Louis, Missouri:
http://www.nps.gov/ulsg

Read a short biography of Julia Dent Grant:
http://www.white.house.gov/WH/glimpse/firstladies/html/jg18.html

Books

Archer, Jules. *A House Divided: The Lives of Ulysses S. Grant and Robert E. Lee.* New York: Scholastic, 1995.

Brash, Sarah. *War between Brothers.* Alexandria, VA: Time-Life Books for Children, 1997.

Diller, Daniel C., and Stephen L. Robertson. *The Presidents, First Ladies, and Vice Presidents: White House Biographies.* Washington, DC: Congressional Quarterly, 1989.

Fitz-Gerald, Christine A. *Julia Dent Grant.* Chicago: Childrens Press, 1998.

Hakim, Joy. *Reconstruction and Reform.* New York: Oxford University Press, 1994.

Marrim, Albert. *Unconditional Surrender: Ulysses S. Grant and the Civil War.* New York: Atheneum, 1994.

Index